A Day in the Park
with Ranger Jack

By Susannah Hartt

A Day in the Park
with Ranger Jack

Copyright © 2013 by Susannah Hartt

All rights reserved.

This book shall not be reproduced in whole or in part,
by any means electronic or mechanical,
without prior written permission from the author.

All illustrations are by Benjamin, Taffy, Jack, and Susannah Hartt
and Sam Wotipka

Additional thanks to
Elora Hartt, Charlie Hartt, Benjamin Hartt, Taffy Hartt,
Lindsay Hartt, Keeter Bailey, Tracey Dobkins, Mark Lunz,
William Ruh, Jaden Tobey, Soni Tobey,
and the campers in site 8

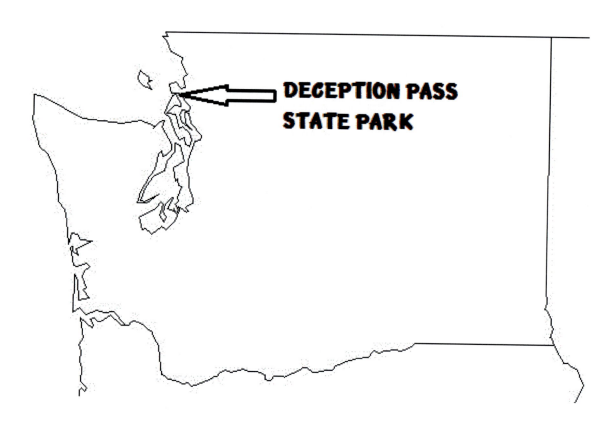

The park is in the northwest corner of the state.

Jack is a park ranger at Deception Pass State Park in Washington State.
Have you been there?

In the morning he puts on a flat hat,
a "Smokey Bear hat",
to show that he is a park ranger.
Visitors know that
rangers are there to help.

He also puts on the same gear that a policeman wears. Part of his job is to protect you and your family when you come to visit the park.

As the sun rises, Ranger Jack raises the flags on a park flagpole.

Jack likes mornings in the park.
The park is coming to life.
He opens the gates to the park,
welcoming the first visitors.

There are many different jobs to be done in a park each day. This morning Ranger Jack helps other rangers in the booth who greet you when you drive into the park.

Jack might need to mow the lawns and pick up garbage today. You won't leave any garbage lying around, will you?

Later, Ranger Jack uses a shovel to dig a hole. He is helping put in a bench at the beach. People will be able to sit here and enjoy the view.

The ranger can tell you about the history of the park or help you find a good trail to hike.

The park has wild places where plants and animals are at home. Ranger Jack helps us protect these special places.

If you earn a junior ranger badge you can help protect the park.

Jack drives through the park in his ranger car. He talks with the campers to make sure everyone is having a good time.

Uh-oh – that car is speeding on the road! Ranger Jack turns on his lights and stops the car. The driver gets a friendly warning.

Ranger Jack likes to talk to people at the beach. People come to the park from all over the world.

There are many special places in the park to discover and explore.

Look at all there is to do in a park. Hiking, swimming, kite flying, canoeing, ...

... fishing, picnicking, camping, bike riding, exploring, or building sandcastles.

There is much work
to be done
in a park, too.
One park worker
is cleaning a
bathroom.

Another is
fixing a roof.

Ranger Jack's radio is calling him.
A man fell off a boat into the water.
The rangers go help rescue the man.

Ranger Jack spends time helping plan for more new campsites in the park.

The campers play all day. In the evening they cook their food over a campfire. A delicious steam rises over the campground!

This family is telling stories around their campfire. Their faces look orange in the firelight.

In this campsite a family is eating s'mores. There is more s'more on their faces than in their mouths!

Four grown ups are laughing
as they play cards by candle light.
Everyone seems so relaxed
and happy after a day in the park.

As it gets dark Ranger Jack takes one last walk through the campground.

Soon the campers are sleeping in their tents or trailers.

Ranger Jack goes home to rest, too.

Made in the USA
Lexington, KY
30 November 2017